Praise for How to Disappear

"Reading *How to Disappear*, I have the sense of someone tearing the past apart and rebuilding with naked raw hands. Claudia Reder is a story teller and this book is her lyrical gift to us, poems of growing up in the teeming city with the complex women who shaped her—immigrant grandmother and mother whose rich mix of languages turned the struggling young girl into a poet who survives to tell their stories. "The list of ghosts / who, no matter where I wander, / who I marry, / who as mother, wife and sister, / haunt me still." These full to bursting poems recreate large, unavoidable terrors and the seemingly small but necessary moments of joy that make art an act of love. They constantly go farther, go deeper with language that is wildly alive, informed by erudite and whimsical exuberance. *How to Disappear* is a splendid book, serious, poetically authentic, spiritually discerning. As I read it, I keep thinking, "This is why I love poetry.""

> —Mary Kay Rummel, Former poet laureate of Ventura County, Author of many books, including *Cypher Garden*, *The Lifeline Trembles*, and *What's Left is the Singing*

"By turns rueful and compassionate, with a touch of magic realism, Reder gathers her mother's life and pours the prickly love that is the legacy she leaves her daughter, into a series of poems filled with the meaningful objects of their lies lived together and apart, vivid colors, umbrellas and uncles, sisters and jewels, and always, stories."

> —Florence Weinberger, Author of numerous poetry collections including *Carnal Fragrance* (Red Hen Press) and *Sacred Graffiti* (Tebot Bach Press)

"The house is burning. / Wherever I step, a new ember" ("The Decision") marks a turning point in Claudia Reder's child-life and is a thread that runs through her collection *How to Disappear* as she delves into family history. "We live like this, / skin sewed onto skin" ("Fable Needing a Moral"): each section links grandmother to mother to daughter in awareness of love, regret, and discovery. While Reder "sing[s] the moon out of me" ("The Night Before Leaving"), her mother is the "keeper of secrets" ("3pm After School My Mother Picks Me Up"). And her grandmother, enduring and memorable Asya, is celebrated to the end: "...you chose abundance.... / You clasped your hands, applauding life" ("Late Night, Lodged on the Corner of the Bed"). *How to Disappear* is a poignant reminder of both the joys and insecurities of childhood and the important choices we make in deciding which memories to keep and which to let go."

—KB Ballentine resides in Chattanooga, Tennessee, where she teaches creative writing, theatre arts, and literature. Her book *The Perfume of Leaving* received the Blue Light Press Book Award. She is the recipient of the Dorothy Sargent Rosenberg Poetry Prize. Her latest book is *Almost Everything, Almost Nothing* (Middle Creek Publishing & Audio).

How to Disappear

Poems by

Claudia M. Reder

BLUE LIGHT PRESS ◆ 1ST WORLD PUBLISHING

1ST WORLD PUBLISHING

SAN FRANCISCO ◆ FAIRFIELD ◆ DELHI

How to Disappear

Copyright ©2019 by Claudia M. Reder

1st World Library
PO Box 2211
Fairfield, IA 52556
www.1stworldpublishing.com

Blue Light Press
www.bluelightpress.com
bluelightpress@aol.com

Book & Cover Art & Design
Melanie Gendron
melaniegendron999@gmail.com

Cover Art
Danny Reder

Author Photo
Claudia M. Reder

First Edition

Library of Congress Control Number: 2018963856

ISBN 9781421838175

Acknowledgments

My Mother's Hats, Breakfast, *Sugar Mule*
My Mother's Voice, *Dirty Napkin*
Portrait of a Latvian Mother, *Adirondack Review*
Imagining Her Death, *Adirondack Review*
To Whom It May Concern:, "Funny is a very complicated issue."
    Poetica Magazine: Contemporary Jewish Writing
Orange, *Uncertain Earth*
Williams-Sonoma, *Passager*
The Meaning of Things, *Arsenic Lobster*
News from Chelm, *Bridges: A Jewish Feminist Journal*
Elegy, *The Healing Muse*
For Dorothy Robbins, Sculptor, *The Healing Muse*
Sunflower, Aunt Betty's Boa, Visit, *Calibanonline*
The Night Before Leaving, *Alaska Quarterly Review*
Finding My Voice, *Calyx*
How to Braid Challah, *Lilith*
Sometimes Truth, *In Posse Review*
Coda, *In Posse Review* (as The Collector and Under the Bridge)
I Will Tell You about the Exhibit of Porcelain Sunflower Seeds
    by Ai Wei Wei, *SPECS journal of art and culture*
Stories from Chelm, *Nimrod*
Wall of Honor, *Jewish Women's Literary Annual*
1060 Park, *Poetica: Reflections of Jewish Thought (titled Threshold)*

Anthologies:
The Lesson, Belmont, Justin Daniel, Ed., *The Art of Bicycling:*
    A Treasury of Poems, Breakaway Books.
March, 1960, Red Blouse (Uscio), *Like Light: 25 years of Poetry & Prose*
    at Bright Hill Press
The Meaning of Things, Perlman, Jim., et al. *The Heart of All That Is:*
    Reflections on Home. Holy Cow! Press, 2013.

Some of these poems were published in the chapbook, *Uncertain Earth*
(Finishing Line Press, 2012).

For my daughter, Miriam
and for my husband, Danny

Table of Contents

I.

March, 1960

I was hiding
when I heard your voice.
Courage grew like a new pair of legs.
I hurried down the stairs!
How long are you staying?
How long would I be safe,
be part of a kite with a flexible string?
I wanted to rise, take in the aerial view.
Was there a way out beyond the poplars?

I was tired of hiding
under my childhood desk
where I didn't fit anymore,
feet scrunched, arms folded.

When my parents yelled
you walked out of the house
and wandered down the suburban street.
I would run after you, my mirror of possibility.
Years later I heard that your husband,
my grandfather —
was the angry one.

I tamp down my own temper.
Imagine what it was like to be a therapist, like you,
still unable to come to grips with anger in the family,
that riptide we spun in.

The Bath

It's not right to bathe with your granddaughter,
my mother's voice, exasperated,
charging you with the crime of me, being twelve,
observing your aging body.

Anger dissolved in the fall of water from the tap
in the deep tub, the aroma of Vitabath embracing our forms,
the prismatic bubbles rainbowing and dispelling
any fear or intimidation my mother wields.

I loved the happy folds of your warm tummy, the relaxed
falling breasts as we sat popping bubbles.

I have read the book about the pigs and horses,
Asya, but how do humans do it?
Asya's hands show me exactly
what goes in and out, and how: vagina and penis.
Why do European men hug each other but not here in America?

Bath, our sacred time, the deep tub, a vessel in which I sail,
Asya, my own beguiling Ms. Frizzle,
tossing taboos out of our protective waters,
allowing me to wonder and question,
curiosity guiding our conversations.

Degas would have first painted the blue mist
wrapping a young girl's form
as she steps over the high-lipped tub
into the dance of her grandmother's arms.

Then he would paint the girl atop the closed toilet seat,
pouting in this compressed space.
A puff of powder springs from her grandmother's
hand. Jean Nate! She laughs.
Only the viewer could intimate
the one discordant blur —
in the doorway the shadow of the rigid mother.

The Day Asya Sits Me in Her Office

I look everywhere, anywhere but at you.
Everything is new: my breasts, my irregular periods,
large red stuffed chairs.
My feet still don't touch the floor.
Am I twelve? Thirteen?

Tell me what's wrong. Talk, please, you have to talk,
your voice rings out.
Whose daughter am I? I want to shout.

The silence between us blows noisy and argumentative.
Your anger steamrolls over me.

Did you buy these
oversized chairs and recover them in vertiginous red patterns
just to make me feel useless and small?

Suddenly the rancor dwindles to human size,
then shrinks, simply a scarf to be folded and tucked in a drawer.
I'm sorry, I should never force anyone to talk. Come.

Your therapist self so badly wanted to help,
but I wanted my grandmother. My Asya is back!
I follow you down the block to our favorite Papaya King.
We noisily suck the cold sweetness through the single straw we share.
I am comfortable again at sea level.
We smile, eye to eye.

Never again would you insist as you had then
when my emerging self stalled.
I chewed on a cuticle and gawked like a fish.

Red Blouse, Uscio

I run an errand, returning something you had borrowed.
I knock on the door you described.
An older man with slobbering lips
invites me into the room, turning
to reach behind him while muttering Italian —

— he grabs me.
He kisses me, forcing the buttons
of my red and white checked blouse,
a blouse I would never remember otherwise. I freeze.
He cups a breast. I utter the only Italian I know —
mi abuelita — mi abuelita.
Suddenly charged, I draw back and run, crying, until you find me.
You and he exchange harsh words in a language foreign to me,
but I understand.

You, the force that protects against chaos,
the buttress against bad things,
are losing your power
which is why we found ourselves at this health spa.
Each morning you drink an herbal concoction
that smells ferocious.
While you swing from doctors, massage, to colonics
I lose myself among the stretch of paths that cut/ twisting
through the promontory overlooking the breathing sea.
I remember uninterrupted cliffs crazy with wildflowers,
red blooms staring up out of dried soil, crags, pebbles.

Your systems had begun to fail.
Among those solitary walks,
I saw death happening in sputters.

I fall over a stubby root, the sky folds in thirds
then quarters, then eighths in its misty layers;
burnt peach brushfire in the sky shadows
the mountain in pink rust.

I hold these vibrant colors in my hands,
wishing you fire and strength.

1060 Park Avenue

The elevator man pushes the brass hinged inside door,
through its patterned diamonds I watch the floors two, three, four.
He stops, adjusts the level several times.
I run out, turn to the right where Asya
tackles me with hugs. I am
shnooksie; my sister, Catrushka;
my mother, Sarinka, or mamushka.
From the kitchen I hear the sounds
of: saran wrap, tin foil, paper bags.
A jar lid falls on the floor as trays are packed
with nova, bagels, chopped liver, challah
that we break off in pieces, never cut with a knife —
and matzoh ball soup from the Madison Avenue deli;
platters of food arrayed on your white linen cloth.

Late Night, Lodged on the Corner of the Bed

How deep was your knowledge of pain,
the nightly visitor that stalked you.
It could be odiferous as skunk,
or an odorless poison;
I would overhear your audible hisses and whispers,
the sharp twinges of neuropathy attacking your legs.

I knew so little of pain then. I would
watch how pain collected your attention
into a bowl of echoes, helpless to stop
its advancement. The next day
my anxiety would reach fever pitch,
as I sprung to the front of the line
for the airplane, the bank; wherever
you needed to be, I would get there early.

By dawn you pushed pain to the outskirts of town
till it distantly swelled on the horizon.
A cloak from childhood swung over your shoulders,
you became the dress you wore, the lipstick, the hair pins,
the therapist, grateful to shoulder another's miseries,
to measure one's life by what one fights for,
to finally reconcile, the generous self slowly taking shape.

Asya, you chose abundance.
Always. For as long as I knew you,
you clasped your hands, applauding life.

Red Daybed

Cocooned by its cluster of brightly woven pillows,
a tapestry of Peruvian alpaca by my head,
tufts of fur to touch when scared.
That summer my attention shifted
to the floor to ceiling wall of books.
I remember where each book sat,
on which shelf, reading greedily
Jung, Adler, *Practicum of Group Therapy*, Wilhelm's *Little Man*
whose cartoons edged me into social consciousness.

I rode the orgone box into the summer equinox
waiting for the dark, opaque and resonant,
to float up through my limbs.
The lustful tones of a trumpet sparked stars.
James Baldwin's sultry summer rooftop parties
seduced me into a New York I didn't know;
rushing through the pages of his novels, my genitals thrummed
to the slow burn of steel drums,
a music exotic and ardent as love. I got lost in the jazz of Harlem.
I analyzed Rorschach inkblots as if they were tarot cards
          affirming my future.

A few years later, at dusk, I turned a street corner
to witness a young woman
who lay down in the middle of rush hour,
her eyes squinting at oncoming headlights.
People directed traffic around her, and I learned
if you blink you might miss the world.

In memory, this room retains its sheltering spirit.
I could descend into reverie, daydream
about the future and argue with myself about the past.

Asya taught me that marriage is hard work,
but once you get to the top
of the mountain the view is beautiful.
Twigs breaking off from their branch
dance all the way to the ground.

Your Office

All eight rooms of your apartment painted cream white
but this one — your office, the inner sanctum,
        walls of muted chocolate.
I always meant to ask why.
I felt I had to whisper as if the act of being here was subversive.
I hadn't yet been initiated into the art of talk.

This was Delphi, gases steamed from the floor,
a chorus of ancient voices of those who had cried out
in anger or betrayal.

Objects transformed into totems: a glass of tea morphed
        into a royal goblet,
the mahogany desk, the flair of its four carved coiled legs,
into Pegasus; the leather-bound calendar, a map of spinning time
able to move forwards and backwards in space.

In this room of mindfulness and rumination,
a wall of books, like a drawbridge, safeguards my reverie.
I learned not to crowd the imagination. Sometimes
I perched at the royal desk and opened
a drawer as if it held invisible ink,
or dared to touch the silver pen
in its metal holder, a ceremonial scepter.

After midnight, in my magical realm, I role played
        therapy sessions.
I tucked myself in the humaness
of one of the thick and plush armchairs,
and listened. A patient spoke to me:
the lonely one who hugged
these dark chocolate walls. The oracle,

grandmother therapist, nodded
to acknowledge the fate of the threadbare
woman and wisely offered her a Mansize box of Kleenex.
Then morning came. My hand smoothed the blanket,
pushed back the chairs, setting the stage for day.

I still want to crawl under the fabric
and touch the shiny lining, my spot of time.

I Study Your Face

We board a boat so you can nap, your head cradled in my lap.
You doze, eyelashes flutter beneath
light blue eyes full of wit.
The tour guide prattles on,
but I am absorbed by your beautiful face,
your masculine features, the chiseled chin, the stolid nose.

We cruise the Portofino shoreline,
the sun-splashed mountains
behind the colorful curve of houses.

Too shy to touch the gracious space
between your eyes, I freely contemplate your unguarded personage.
I note your slim ankles. I want to rub away their pain.
Your small hands, the large garnet and coral rings,
the fine coastline of your brows;
the numerous secrets they shutter.

Now your eyes open, you are dazed,
I must have had too much wine, you say.
You sit up straight to realign your thoughts,
looking like a cubist portrait
Picasso would smooth to become your face.

Gingerbread House

In Asya's well-lit apartment I am the center of attention,
But she needs to make a call.
At Elk's Candy she purchases the largest Gingerbread House.
Do you think they'll like it?
I nod my head, What's not to like?
Inside a newly polished building I press the elevator's silver button.

A doleful woman and man open their apartment door,
Christmas carols sing quietly from a radio.
A crumpled Kleenex in her hand, the unnamed woman
stands beside a Christmas tree.
They marvel at the jellybean doorways, corn candy roof;
Asya in the doorway, blows kisses for both cheeks.

I wasn't meant to be part of the scene.
True to the Hippocratic oath Asya cannot divulge
the reason for their bold grief.
I invent scenarios. They had lost their child, or,
desperately hoped for one? Why else would a whimsical
Gingerbread House cheer them so?

Asya could take an orange and present it as a mystery.
From then on, the mystery of an orange
was something to delight in.

Asya, the enchantress, wanding the air with her gift,
could lift the mood of any room,
I am still astonished.

Family Portrait c. 1910, Russia

This formal Russian family portrait
has been rescued, digitized and resized:
eight siblings, bookended by a stern mother
and a regal father in his vest and top hat.

Esther, the oldest, dressed as a man to attend medical school.
Anna became a nurse. When Anna volunteered
        at the Russian Front
she didn't know she would bring home Esther's casket.
Did Oskar die on the front or from cancer?
Was his name Oskar? Who is the other brother?
What happened to Zena's happiness?

Eleanor, Anna's only daughter,
will die in her twenties, on a Los Angeles
corner run down by a motorcyclist.
I hold one of her gloves, the lace rigid with age.
On reading a college paper she wrote on puppetry
I think I miss you. We would have gotten on.

I stand back from the photo to note the formal dress
and bodices of the young women, their high buttoned-up
necks, their long tresses nestled at their waists.

Betty gambled and partied. In her eighties,
she stood on her bed in a slip and boa,
said it was her summer dress and opened the door for a stroll.

At the center of the photo, Asya, the young one, age eight,
has a wisp of a smile. She will shop in Paris for shoes,
regale to Vienna, study psychology and become my grandmother.

First they will find themselves at the edge of a field
        waiting to be shot.
Then they must find their way out of Europe.

Their thick wild hair combs through mountains,
gets stuck on fence poles,
these women whose long thick hair I touch
as if my own glossy curls.

Rachmaninoff's 2nd Piano Concerto

(This concerto was dedicated to the physician who had helped
him through several years of depression)

The root chords begin their musical journey,
an oarsman tosses an oar hopeful a listener will catch it.
The weight of its rounded wood lands in my palm.

I listen, cradled in the chords, chromatics soar,
overtones of unrest, then in a surge of passion,
 images rush out, as large as life:

the chair I sat in in my grandmother's office,
the thick rings she wore to hide her thick fingers,
my small hands that could not stretch far enough on the keyboard;

the red daybed, the coiled dark wood table,
the leather notebook, pen in its metal holder;
hand prints all over the paper, for my brazen grandmother,

my awkward mother, my lefthanded daughter.
We emerge, triumphant
among the numinous sadnesses.

2.

Portrait of My Mother

Yours is the upside-down Cinderella story,
the wealthy young girl caught in the vortex
of the Holocaust. In New York City at eighteen
you hadn't yet learned how to boil water.

It was your fate to marry a Depression boy,
on your way to Ph.D.s.

Money, one argument among many.
After the divorce, you grudgingly budgeted,
maintained an elegant apartment, stylish clothing,
high European manners, the essence
of the woman who had arrived at Manhattan.
Your lifestyle exacted a cost.

You sold the family stocks, a gold cigarette case,
a Käthe Kollwitz sketch to put your daughters through college,
slept on a long narrow couch in the living room.
The one bedroom was sacred for your daughters' occasional visits,
beds made, The Supremes on the turntable.
I sat next to you, just to touch.
But you had grown armored and didn't hug much.

After your mother, Asya, died, I saw my therapist one more time.
Picture the upper East Side office, low lights, brown leather
        ottomans.
One thing you should know, your mother may be suicidal.
I flash on the collection of pills in your cabinet.

Should I stay? Should I go?
No, he replied, *go to school*.

Apparently I inherited depression
That would come and go like an emotional flu.

3pm After School My Mother Picks Me Up

Mama swallows. The tight line of her mouth
accentuates her high cheekbones.
I forget to notice how pretty she is.
Her angry eyes snap violet.

We drive home to the restless cherry tree biding its time,
the runt of a peach tree that never blossoms,
to poplars, the tallest vertical for miles,
separating one green yard from another.

As I've aged, we mirror each other
in ways we don't expect. I inherit
the deep blue and purple rings
that swell beneath my mother's eyes.

She speaks in metaphor,
wraps words around her fingers,
lets nuance radiate.
My mother, keeper of secrets
had been trained in sorceress' riddles:

It's not a daughter's right to look into her mother's soul.
I have bars on my heart.

Now that I'm a mother I pencil in her hurt.
I imagine a conversation we never had.
She will answer my unasked question,
Your father yelled a lot. I didn't know what to do when he yelled.
We would hug across the tonal distances,
across the poplars that shadowed my early years.

The Decision

Atop my bed's pink nubby coverlet,
my mother tries to explain:
divorce. The word that invaded
their nightly arguments
now stood upright.

At my second-floor window, I lift the window shade.
I imagine tulip bulbs quiet and closed beneath their soil,
the tiger lily and iris bed awaiting spring.

Who do you want to live with? mother asks.
Where are you going?
New York. I have a job there.

Father stays. He plants
tulip bulbs, weeds the dry patch of the peach tree.

How can I choose
between mother's fiery violet eyes, or father,
a mysterious frightening stranger?

From friends, therapists, doctors,
"let the child choose."
Could I choose neither
and desire both?
I back into the safety of my room.

Had I known this decision
would follow me, had I known
what awaited, I would not have chosen this.

The rift between my mother and I
would resonate in so many ways.
You would not be swayed.
That angry, decisive night still fires up
in recurring dreams. The house is burning.
Wherever I step, a new ember.

For years afterwards
as college students raced for independence
I chose to go home — finally
home and lived with you.

My Mother at Seventy

Wintry New York City streets. We tramped through slush
and gritty sidewalks.
Your legs were good then. There, a restaurant where you a
single woman
comfortably ate. There, Rockefeller Center where you
ice-skated and broke your wrist;
there, the travel agent who helped you find the best rates
for my college loans.
Born in Riga, Latvia, you would not speak your mother tongue
when visiting Germany. What happened to your mamaloshen?
You would offer only, *Riga Beach. It had the whitest sand.*
You lived across from the circus, the Cirque Riga, the oldest
in the world. I imagine a meandering boulevard along the park;
along this magnificent route you lived.

"It's your father's birthday. Did you send him a card?"
Divorced many years, he is still a safer subject than your homeland.
"Yes," I mutter. I had bought it. I just haven't sent it
and don't remember where I put it. At that moment
the air is brown and green like the two colors of his eyes.
I am sitting in the middle of his head.

A memory: you have locked yourself in the bathroom.
He kicks at and punches the door.

"And your sister, you love your sister, right?"
"Of course I love my sister."
"I love you, too," I quickly add, but you have turned away.

Is it because you were raised by strict German governesses?
Because your twin sister died at age eight of a bad heart?
When she died her skin color was no longer blue, it was
        your natural white.

Wealthy beyond what I could ever imagine, you grew up among
cooks, maids, and with a professional mother. You shared one
story — which I cherish.
You were twelve. To see your ever-absent mother you made
     an appointment

through her secretary. Dressed in your Russian hat,
skirt and silk blouse, white gloves and small purse, you wait.
Asya opened the door.
"I wanted to see you," you said.
Was Asya in shock? Or did she enjoy the irony of the situation,
Asya, the prankster?
When I was five, you outfitted me as a cowgirl complete with boots,
a Daniel Boone hat and tiny guns that popped caps.
Foreign objects reflected your new love of America, but I felt closer
to your stories of Tsars, pogroms, the Romanov sisters,
     who was the real
Anastasia, (so many movies!), the Winter Palace, and the mystery
of the Amber Room, its gold leaf and jewels, amber walls,
     stolen by Nazis.

Now that amber fills with secrets of you and your mother,
     things I will never know.
Here is sunlight that has hardened, yellow orange, the unrest
     of amber.
Taste its warm fur like brandy in my mouth.

My Mother's Hats

The angrier Daddy got, the more he spat,
spewing crows, feathers and caws, children crying,
mother dodging the angry plumes,
swallowing a few, giving breath to others.

You learned to wear your elegance
and lack of self-confidence
in daring hats flocked with these extraordinary feathers:
magenta quills, orange barbs, a peacock's
glaring eye, each hat neatly stored in its round box
on the top closet shelf. Hats for summer,
or stormy weather, for unexpected drafts.

You grew more beautiful as you aged,
the grand dame at the café,
sipping a Pernod, ready for any occasion.

Breakfast

One morning my mother
wakes, a crocodile,
able to walk on two legs,
serving orange juice.
I ask for milk for my cereal.
She strolls to the table
before dressing stylishly for work,
arranging the skirt so the slip
won't show, selecting
a flowered blouse with a high
neck to cover the wrinkly
throat, and ruby earrings
that glint in the light
so that her colleagues would eye
their shimmer, mistaking
beauty for happiness.

Fable Needing a Moral

My mother sews herself up tight.
I wear her on my arm,
a strapping alligator bag.

It really is not my style, I rebuff,
but her response is to yawn,
and transpose my shoes into
matching alligator boots.

We live like this,
skin sewed onto skin,
the family glue dried clear.

My Mother's Voice

is green, radiates elegance and splendor.
Even when she must live frugally, laughs larkspur,

If you don't leave the house, you spend less.
When I was a child her voice frightened me
as if alive with a shark's radiant power.

My mother's voice sings citrus —
joie de vivre á l'orange,
the tone I depended on
as a teen to lift me from depression.
Suicide is a waste of time, she'd say,
We don't have time for nervous breakdowns.

Sometimes my mother's amethyst voice answers the phone,
You're the only one who calls, she says.

When I ask her a question about our difficult past,
she responds, Oh, is that cobra raising its ugly head again?
Today her elbows on the wheel chair arms,

one hand rests on her forehead.
She conducts a concert of hands,
of waving, nail biting, wringing hands.
She hasn't seen her husband in over forty years,

but I notice they have similar expressions
as if they had grown old together in the same room.

Portrait of a Latvian Mother

Broad wrists
struggle with gold chains;

brown marks, not moles or freckles,
she says, just spots. She's some leopard,
hair like sifted brown flour.

We don't often touch,
not like my grandmother and I astride the hammock,
my short leg balanced against her longer one.

The clasp of a gold chain caught
in my mother's hair, I untangle the wispy strands,
I touch the bald spaces.

She lightly pats my hair, saying,
You're lucky, you have such thick hair.
I rub her sweaty scalp.

She smells good,
like something I'd like to touch
and breathe in: remembering

her chestnut hair swooped into a bun,
scooped neck dress to show off
the fine slope of her shoulders.

I zip her dress, she talks,
If you hadn't given up playing piano,
she shakes her head. All that music.

She sighs. What she wants
to say is lost in those moments
when she sat to listen to me

play her favorite composers:
Rachmaninoff, Beethoven, or Brahms.

Cranberry Kissel

The sweet cranberry soup at the Russian Tea Room,
the warm thick cream I order
when my mother takes me out
to dine on blini and kissel
and discuss how I want to live with my boyfriend
in her apartment for a few weeks.
After getting over the shock
she says, well, the red daybed is all she has,
and perhaps if we two sleep head to toe, we can manage.
I give her kisses, and am pleased,
the warm kissel in my mouth,
sweet red fruit of pleasure.

A decade later she will meet the man I marry.
We three dine at a steak house although he is vegetarian,
but here she holds court, an elegant red hat sweeps over her brow.
The owner Walter in his long black cape
leans over to offer a gallant kiss. She proffers
the role of a grand Russian lady
who stands in front of the sun.

To Whom It May Concern:

My mother has moved into her room at Nouvelle Gardens
where her window, overlooking a quiet courtyard,
distresses her. Please provide a city view
with the clatter of pedestrians,
traffic, a car horn. Place the sunflower quilt
right side up on her bed, and light
the room with the matching Van Gogh print.

We must rethink the bathroom, too, the shower seat.
How much more of her life can we give away
while malady whittles one memory, use of an arm?
We forge one house into a tiny closet, her love
of fine China traded in for paper plates,
bibs, and a Kleenex stuffed into her sleeve.
We hope she can still wheel herself
to the window to look out,
but the wheel chair might catch
on the bed post, or she might
not be able to push. Please check on her.
She likes blintzes, and once in a while,
could you share your rugelach?
Please fix her cable tv, tune it to CNN,
daily, Anderson Cooper, her boyfriend.
Remember, missed opportunities will swarm at her feet
while she sleeps on the thickness of fevered pine needles
aware of the world in all its Weltschmerz,
and her escape into its invisible music.

Aunt Betty's Boa

We're on our way to the Hotel Ansonia to visit this
        rumpled Russian aunt.
She and my mother switch smoothly from Yiddish, Russian,
        German.

Later I ask my mother, Out of all your aunts, you like Aunt Betty?
Oh yes, she laughs with no strings attached. Aunt Betty was fun.

I won't hear this spontaneous giggle again until my mother
        is very old,
in a wheel chair, and I hold her hands, and we dance.

It's hard to imagine mother adorned with a boa, her aunt's
        arm in hers,
in Russia or Riga, dressed to the nines. But I like thinking
she could have been happy once, even in love, out until dawn.

Evening

Mountains surround me.
Trakl, what do you want me to see
in these milky hills?

I lie down beside my mother
in this changeable landscape,
sip from Gull Pond.

My mother has taken on the strength of a dying woman.
She propels herself slowly.
Sometimes she appears to stand still.

As she moves forwards
I look backwards
and listen to the white of evening.

Orange

When my mother dies I purchase
an orange tea kettle
and cook with her orange Creuset pots
that counterscape my kitchen.
I dream her. She appears in that rift
between us as if it were a locale I am obliged to visit
amid the scent of a young onion.
The whip of egg whites
slaps the sides
of the shiny copper bowl.

In a cloud of steam
my mother raises her spoon
to taste the beef bourguignon
laced with burgundy,
or to sample the scampi.
She tucks the scallops St. Jacques
inside their clam shells.

Today I lift her seasoned wooden spoon
above the steaming lentils,
ready to add a touch of vinegar.
Forgiveness stirs the broth.

Williams-Sonoma

Because I've given away her silver and fine kitchen bakeware
to my brother-in-law and his husband who swore
while emptying her kitchen that it was like shopping
at a private party at Williams-Sonoma,
my mother is acting out.

She leaves a peach scent from the nightgown
that lies in the blue dresser drawer.
We had shopped specially
for the night jacket when her mother had entered Mt. Sinai.
We also purchased lace handkerchiefs embroidered with tiny
            blue flowers.

At the ocean sipping espresso, watching the pink fine lines of sun
splitting cloud from island, island from sky,
sky from horizon,

the full moon, transparent as an ice cube
I can lift with a silver tong.

The Meaning of Things

First it was her purses she wondered about, then
the silver soup spoons, then back to purses.
One day, out of the blue — her umbrellas —
as if having these items back again
would give meaning to her life —
"a wheel chair life."
Her words.

Anxiety grows. "Who put these things in this room,
the one I live in now?" Wondering, "How did I get here.
Tell me again, how it happened, the stroke."

And I would tell again how it happened,
how we moved her and by phone she told us
what she wanted and didn't want;
how my sister and I had to make choices,
how we didn't think she'd need umbrellas.
How we gave away her stylish clothes.

At least we didn't put everything in a dumpster
like another family she knows. Losing
control, she demands: "Where are my things?"
By this, she means her life, the flotsam
and jetsam of accidents, emergencies,

a random design of nature. Here you are mother,
here, in this chair, here are your arms, mother,
push, push. Let the past go.
"I have only one regret,"
she says, "but meanwhile, Where are my things?"

News from Chelm

This small candle in a glass
    begins my worry
that the prayer will not even tap the ceiling
nor seep through
    the drafty window.
I blow it out
to appease my mother who is afraid
the house will burn down.

Even at Chanukah, the watched menorah
candles swiftly burn to ash
so we can get to bed early.
So how do we mourn?

Ozick says, *Though English is my everything, now and then
I feel cramped by it.*

Trained under the ear of a speech therapist mother,
I wonder how to put that inflection
back into my English,
put the tsauris back into the single language

I was taught.
We're in America now.
Why do you want to do that?

English is my everything, says Ozick,
And my mind is filled with phrases I am homesick for,
gestures amiss without their vocal choreography.

I turn to folktales of Chelm.
In Chelm, Yiddish is spoken. In Yiddish,
you can say sentences,

saying one word
and gesturing another. In Yiddish there is always a story.

To live in Chelm is to be in love with commas,
to punctuate your speech with "and," "so?"
Share your angst with "Ach" over tea.

    I read the tales to my mother.
Hah! She retorts.
    That story doesn't make sense.
Her forehead crinkles. She counts
pearl, knit, pearl. Knit.
        It reminds me of your Aunt Anna.
        She was supposed to visit her sister
for one week. She arrived and never left.

I can't quite unravel the leap.
My mother's thought loops around
the lost circuits of Chelm,
between German, Yiddish,
Russian, English,
angst, and who knows what
        other secrets she keeps hidden
        in her unfinished afghans.

Oh, that chameleon, language, that
        colors and blemishes our remembering.

It doesn't seem valid to compose a sonnet
to explain these linguistic flights,
feathers flying off when least expected.

They land on the sill
and in my palm, others tickle.
We are our own Chelm stories,
our truth embedded in a transmutation
of ourselves, as we light the Yahrzeit.

Elegy

Riga, 1939,
the table set for dinner,
the family simply walked out
towards America.

Now my mother grows too close to the house.
Let the aromas of foods she loves circulate
to the tips of her leaves.

Let her anxieties rest.
Let this tree honor stillness
of dry summer nights.
At the heartwood

I catch my breath.
Against her tilted
and muscular trunk

my husband and I toast with a glass of dry wine.
He parses the orb of an orange,
hands me one manageable slice at a time.

Sunflower

The evening my mother returns from the hospital,
flowers close their multiple petals.

She lies on the couch.
In the red moment of poppies,
she stretches out her one good arm.
I think about the strange hands that change her,
wipe her, bathe her, hand her the phone.

Standing among sunflowers
she becomes a sunflower.
Her shadow lengthens,
slender as a street lamp.

She is the window overlooking the East River,
she is the sunset off the Hudson.

In this moment the horizon is a portal;
somewhere a sprig of flower
blossoms into a live woman.

3.

The Night Before Leaving

The night before
leaving for boarding school
I sing the moon out of me,

the moon and the house,
the moon, the house, the yelling
embedded in the arms of the living room chairs,

the moon, the house, the yelling,
and the whole backyard
where I would squat in the grape

arbor hidden by large flat leaves
filled with purple grapes
so sour and full of minuscule

seeds no one would eat them.
The beautifully stained
purple brick under my feet,

I sing the moon, the house,
I sing the moon, the house,
the grape arbor, and the dining room picture

window where I hum my reveries,
and the tension muted by the thick gold rugs,
the hushshshs, I take the hussshshsh.

Geometry

Housemother, Mrs. D. labels me anti-social
and teaches geometry.
I like the security of shapes,
the puzzle of fractals,
one symmetrical form fitting into another,
tetrahedron upon tetrahedron.

During a long bus ride with my mother
to Niagara Falls
to stand beneath the roar of water
in a yellow poncho
an old man on the seat behind me
reveals the secrets
of my book's illustrated
directions: I learn to fold a crane:
peak folds, valley folds,
and how to turn the tip of paper
inside out to form a beak. From straws,
I construct octagons and decahedrons
to hang from the ceiling like planets;
I will stray from such useless magic.

Boredom

I'm afraid you'll be bored,
my writing teacher says
when I select a small
progressive college in the woods:
no grades, departments, classrooms.

Bored? Perhaps she confused
my depressed visage with boredom.

Guys who avoid the draft
shoot pool, smoke, drink —
desperate, but not bored;

tucked inside depression's shell,
unable to imagine my favorite color —
Blue? Green? Likes, dislikes?
I prefer not to choose.

I dream college will be
an artist's colony
tucked in the woods.

If I major in basket weaving
I could travel to Indonesia
to study style and design,
or Thailand to study ritual dance.

But I never leave the northeast:
Providence, Rhode Island,
New York.

Winters in Vermont
I hang out
at the weaving barn,
chat in sunlit studios,
applaud these makers,

buy itchy handmade pillows
to lie against in bed.

Something askew,
not boredom.

I lean against a hallway wall,
book of poetry in hand,
a professor permits me
in my hiking boots
and long silk skirts
to read and write, *It's a valid life.*

At a booth in the dining hall,
we work through my hermetic
drafts. *Trust your images.*
Don't explain them. She
compares my work to early Merwin.
Like him, parts of you dismembered
appear in the ocean.

Senior year she says,
I don't know how you did it,
but these are poems, and walks off
in oval reading glasses
and common sense
black pants and shirt.

Finding My Voice

The professor stammers,
The problem is…
well, you write like an immigrant.
Oh! I sit up straight. My mother's Latvian.
His face reddens, but he has stirred my poem-roots,
the speech inflection of those who say,
"Get it for me, the bread,"
and, "If you don't eat it, the cake,
then you don't love me."
Pronouns and nouns inverted
until I was not sure which was which.
At home German was spoken
when grown ups didn't want children to understand.
I learned to consciously listen
to how the mouth shapes itself,
to the guttural umphs, and open 'aah's!
each with its own hand gestures.
My grandmother would enter a room
chin first, like an exclamation point,
when saying, "Sarinka,"

Body language filled in for lost words.
Words that could not be retrieved in English
could be found in French, Italian, Russian,
German, or some dramatic beckoning.
English was a paltry language,
like Chef Boyardee spaghetti eaten cold
out of the can when they first immigrated
and lived in hotels. The spice of language
was alive in the drama of Dostoyevsky,
the pathos of language in Chekhovian afternoons.
We knew how quickly each event

could turn into a dire emergency
and a need for a hot glass of tea.
Tea and pauses created room for stories,
stories that wandered here and there,
interrupted by phone calls, errands,
or a patient waiting for his time slot.
In and out of life was conversation,
beguiling, begun, never ending,
pronouns, nouns, tossed
like afghans, thrown with kisses.

Because I love the caesura —
the space where words are spent,
the interval in which one hunts
for the next word
and sometimes can't find it,
the pause in which one hugs
while searching the room
for a noun, a verb,
or a familiar face —
(not knowing an idiom
never prevented us from talking) —
I became a poet.

"Funny is a very complicated issue."
— Wendy Wasserstein

My immigrant grandmother
and great aunts orbit the periphery,
their voices thick and accented like a Russian stew.

When I'm twelve, I realize
theater conveys stories I hadn't dared tell;
theater is one place where I'm allowed to feel.

When the sink clogs on Thanksgiving
and the bills have been accidentally paid twice,
which is why no money sits in the account;

my daughter and I spy a coyote
chasing a chicken up the gravelly hill
in a flurry of fleeing, and wings that balk.
Months later, we're still rooting for the chicken.

Funny keeps gravity under our feet
and our neuroses compatible.
Like poetry, it cannot be paraphrased.

When a friend read this poem,
she said, *But it's not funny.*
It is not meant to be, I reply.

An oncologist hugs his patient
before she sets off to Patagonia.
Bundled up, she smiles, peering
out from a glacier,
hanging at the edge of chaos;
funny means when we're deadly serious,
we channel comedy.

How to Braid Challah

I. Ingredients

You will be baking
with languages.
Russian, German,
and Yiddish
will suffice —
but contain
large quantities
of gluten —

II. Mixing the Dough

While you
knead the flour and yeast,
gathering strength
in your arms
and volume
in your voice,
such heated
discussions
until the children
scream, Stop arguing!
and you retort
we are not arguing.
We are discussing
Aunt Ruthie
and your lost tooth
and Rachel's
report card
and Zena's last
doctor's appointment

for TMJ
slap slapping down
turn turning it over
in the dough —
your conversations
rise, conflate.
And because
your temper
has risen
just a bit —
you might be in danger
of braiding
the challah
too tightly —
be mindful.

III. Cutting and Braiding

When cutting
the dough
into three, four, six
braids, they may be
too long for the
counter space.
Feel free to use the old-
fashioned mahogany
dining room table —
or linoleum —
whatever you've got
will do. Stretch
out the lengthy ropes.
Take up room.
English sentences
are famished
for intonation,

complexity,
and desire.

Using generous hand
motions, braid
the pogroms.

Don't forget to flour
the board every so often —
sweeping your hand
across the marble,
a clean slate.

IV. Optional

Brush with egg
white twice
so the loaves glisten —
once after
braiding
and again after
baking

in honor
of your
Russian
grandmother
who threw two
kisses, one
for each cheek;

or sprinkle
a Yinglish
of raisins,
or poppy seeds.

V. Serving the Challah

Invite oodles of people.
Tear off chunks.

Dance with your bread.

Let the crumbs
fall on the good table
cloth, so be it.

For Dorothy Robbins, Sculptor

i.

Girl on a Fence,
eight inches tall, cast in bronze, sits on a sill.
We look out of the same window.
She straddles the present, my past,
and the marvel of daydream.

I am ten.
I am the girl on the fence,
wrapped up in books.
I read Chekhov's biography,
then go for Catullus. Not understanding what I read
the words glide by on their own slopes.

After school I hike down the hill
to the Carnegie Library
whose halls echo like a grand ballroom
under my loafers. I nod to Egyptian Gods,
Mesopotamian pillars,
and two marble lions before climbing
the wide staircase to the adult reading room
where I reach for the novel hidden behind the shelves.

ii.

Girl Holding an Owl,
chiseled from a single block of wood,
always stands near my front door.
After my parents' divorce,
this three-foot high guardian
became my dream image,

an owl with eyes like searchlights
whose wing span fends off nightmares
from the woodpecker tapping each dawn
at my bedroom rotting wooden window frame,
to the drawing of a house my grandmother
asked me to make for her every so often.

iii.

When muscular dystrophy made it impossible
for you to carve wood, or cast bronze,
you sculpted with wax.
You found your way.

Paper is my sky;
words are my dreaming;
This poem is for you, Dottie.
I affirm: whatever we are dealt, we will still create,
transform, and offer to the world
our delicate, vulnerable shapes.

Sometimes Truth

Sometimes truth arrives
on a white donkey,
limping, heartbroken with hunger;

I offer the donkey water.
It sips appreciatively and noisily
out of the wide mouth cup.

His lean skull gleams
through his wrecked hide, a sliver
of moon nips a jagged hoof,

and suddenly, memories light
between my two fingers
just as I unlock the front door.

I Will Tell You about the Exhibit of Porcelain Sunflower Seeds by Ai Wei Wei

At first you think they are real seeds,
but these are porcelain sunflower seeds
each painted by hands that have touched

centuries of pottery in this small town.
Their beauty is unexpected,
you walk among them, rake them,

hold one in your palm, while you consider
how many visitors held this particular seed,
how old the hands that held the paint brush.

For Ai Wei Wei, art was warfare.
After some time, the seeds
were found to release a toxin

so that the museum goers were no longer
allowed to play among them, but only
to stand behind a rope and gaze at them.

Art is dangerous, after all.

Stories from Chelm

i.

Is there such a town in Poland named Chelm?
Yes, but I am not from that Chelm.
I am from the Chelm of stories.

ii.

Who knew the moon could get lost?
In the dark round of the barrel, the full moon glittered
like a huge latke with enormous flaky edges.

iii.

In the waiting room for displaced persons,
one woman kneads her hands.
She knows if the challah doesn't rise
she must throw it out and start over.

iv.

Each night in Chelm, as people prepare for bed,
they place their shoes facing the same direction
so that on waking they will know which way to go.

v.

Remember Saul who thought he was in love with your mother?
He had given up his love of the clarinet to become a lawyer,
        like his father.
One day at a bus stop, he is so tired he leaves his feet
and comes back for them the next day.
Then he gets cancer, dies; only forty-five.
Why do I tell you this story? It's like they say in Chelm,
his shoes got turned around and so he walked into the wrong life.

v.
Grief does that,
makes whole parts of you fall off
when you aren't looking.

Learning Salsa

Laying his hands on my hips,
the Jamaican man said, "Let go,
the rhythms will guide you."

I asked him to tell me stories
because to those cadences I could fall asleep.

I wore my light brown dress
that twirled at the knee
tenting as I spun my way
towards a sacred meditation
that never happened,
even when I spun
in the opposite direction
to unspool whatever energy
had gathered
on my heated skin.

I stopped to observe the subtle
changing stained glass rose windows,
the strains of music
that lifted into the vaulted
ceiling of the church,
dancing at St. John of the Divine.

"Oh, now you're getting it," the Jamaican man
smiled, pulling me tighter, letting me go,
bobbing along the floor to gentle congas and horn.

That's as close as I ever came to the exhilaration
of a leap, to the taste of air
at the top
of the warm room,
to a dance that neared prayer,
to a prayer that could
carry me.

The Lesson

Stand next to your bike, like that,
says my father, holding the new Minox camera
that fits in his shirt pocket. I am a chubby ten,
in profile, the worst, my too tight shirt
over tight stretch pants, holding onto the handle bars.
How many lessons will it take?

In Atlantic City my mother rents a bike. I practice
on the board walk, children whizzing past,
age five or six. To compensate,
my mother stuffs a giant bear in my arms.

The bear is blue, the bike is blue, the sky is blue,
and I cannot ride, I cannot ride, my fingers
grip bars that are supposed to hold me
and do not. My feet turn pedals
that are supposed to take me somewhere
and they do not.

At twenty-four, in graduate school,
I practice on a rusty blue bike
my boyfriend found in a park after rain.
He holds the back and lets go.
I think, I can do this,
but each time I feel the surge of power,
I waver and shout,
I'm going to crash into that tree, and I do.

The Visit

If anyone knows how to grieve, Demeter does.
She grieves head on.
Stretched out on my natty, blue couch,
her ashy clothes flare,
her face riddled with danger and rudeness.
I massage her swollen feet.

Have you seen Persephone, she asks? She was here earlier, I reply.
Demeter takes it in stride,
much like a shade of my mother
who was also standoffish.

Her gold belt corroded, she still desires
sonograms of Persephone's future children.

Her cuticles bleed.
How human. She has been chewing on them.
She has given up sandals
for boots with mirrored soles.
I notice a toe missing.

I lace her boots. She knots her belt.
I take her hand.
Yoked with ropes and axes
we ferry our chorus of burdens
across the glowing hills.

Imagining Her Death

Asya stands beside
the large crystal edged mirror that reflects
the black leather footstools, the aqua leather chairs,
the much used ash trays of her living room.
Her evening therapy group asks,
What are you doing?
She replies, *I want to see*
what you look like without me.

Basket of Red Leaves

My neighbor, a rickety old man,
who each morning collects red, fallen leaves
in his yard with long pincers, scales the porch
stairs in fragile slippers where he spills
the leaves into a large basket, the fresh
red ones atop the brown edged crumbles.
Over time the basket of leaves smells
like the bad breath of gods.

Wild

Emily, pull your creased shorts
out of your crotch, hold out your skinny arms,
sing and jabber about nothing
while you straddle the log above the stream
pretending it is five feet high.

Jane, laugh as we push each other off
the burnt branch that wobbles
like a horse that could hold all of us;
bouncing on a lightning struck
tree, we could pretend anything.

Wrestling with ferns, we run back and forth
over the same places until they are worn
and comfortable. We tame
the wild on that steep hill
of woods tilted towards the sky.

Coda

Stepping lightly on the earth's
spongy tongue, I breathe its fragrant
breath of weeds and rot,
expectant: listening for crickets,
leaves that tremble with bird droppings.

Dreamless nights I drive without stopping
for street lights, wanting to wipe
a name from the list of ghosts
who stop by every so often.

I grew up ghost-fed along the edges of the damp
and the wet-wet, lip synching bird calls
until the dune driven winds
were sidelined by spring
light engulfing the feverish soil
along the frog fed banks.

Under the bridge in a watery
troll's reflective glare,
my mother's all-knowing eyes
rise from grief's spiky adagio
of wrecked seaweed, a hiccup
at the glimmer of her mouth.

A heron uprooted from its favorite
turf returns to its favored
fence post, third down from the elm,
the one I had straddled long afternoons
as a daydreaming teen.

Here I am, years later, ghost riding
into the moonlit soaked spaces
narrowing between us,
wings flapping.

One Childhood is Not Enough

The tree burns blue in our minds
and red in our dreams.
During the day the odor of smoke
follows us, we wake to a dream-image of danger.

It takes so much to live in this world.
The years, shredded leaves, under my feet.

My mother is the size of a doll,
ten inches high, in my hand.
She is standing,
and I say fly, mother, fly,
as she lifts into the air.

Another day, she appears squat with her bundles and bags.
She suffers back and shoulder aches
unable to fit her whole self into that forced shape
of her marriage.

Something fills my pockets.
From each pocket a bird lifts into the sky.
Their wings beat furiously
to reach that blue freedom.

Wall of Honor

Mother, you and I mill among tourists and vendors
selling Dove ice cream bars. It is hot even for June,
a beautiful day to be near the Sound.
Suddenly, you clutch my arm. Did you trip? Feel faint?
But you whisper, *It's just as it was.*

We lose and find each other in the Great Hall,
get our bearings in the gift shop,
before we climb polished stairs,

gaze at the array of children's shoes:
red Chinese silk, Turkish embroidered;
brown oxfords even I recognize.

You cry out,
Ach, look, my father had one just like that!
I look where you look: the tefillin
from your private store of memories.

In the Main Hall I photograph wicker luggage,
baskets, and other paraphernalia of arrival.

Outdoor, near the sea wall —
we locate your mother's name —
    Asya —
but not your father's —
you hadn't had it engraved.
He never really wanted to come, you say,
He was never the same.

You left Latvia at age eighteen.
At the sea wall I touch your name.

About the Author

Claudia M. Reder is the author of *Uncertain Earth* (Finishing Line Press) and *My Father & Miro* (Bright Hill Press). She has received the Charlotte Newberger Poetry Prize from *Lilith Magazine*, selected by Alicia Ostriker. She has a passion for helping other people tell their stories. She has an M.F.A. from the Iowa Workshop and a Ph.D. in Storytelling from New York University. For many years she was a poet in the Schools on the east coast and has offered many workshops for all ages in creativity. She teaches at California State University at Channel Islands.

www.ingramcontent.com/pod-product-compliance
Lightning Source LLC
Chambersburg PA
CBHW032026090426
42741CB00006B/748